GERMAN SLANGUAGE

A *FUN* VISUAL GUIDE TO GERMAN TERMS AND PHRASES BY MIKE ELLIS

DEDICATED TO ALL THOSE WHO THOUGHT LEARNING GERMAN WAS DIFFICULT.

First Edition
17 16 15 14 13   5 4 3 2 1

Text © 2013 Mike Ellis
Illustrations © 2013 Rupert Bottenberg,
except illustration of heart on page 45,
© maximma/Shutterstock.com

Published by
Gibbs Smith
P.O. Box 667
Layton, Utah 84041

1.800.835.4993 orders
www.gibbs-smith.com

Designed by michelvrana.com

Gibbs Smith books are printed on paper produced
from sustainable PEFC-certified forest/controlled
wood source. Learn more at www.pefc.org.
Printed and bound in Hong Kong

Library of Congress Cataloging-in-Publication Data

Ellis, Mike, 1961–
  German slanguage : a fun visual guide to German
terms and phrases / Mike Ellis. — 1st ed.
     p. cm.
  ISBN 978-1-4236-3192-7
1. German language—Conversation and
phrase books—English. I. Title.
  PF3121.E67 2013
  438.3'421—dc23
                                    2012031240

CONTENTS

HOW TO USE THIS BOOK

If you have always wanted to learn the basics of German, but traditional methods seemed overwhelming or intimidating, this book is for you! Just follow the directions below and soon you'll be able to say dozens of words and phrases in German.

• Follow the illustrated prompts and say the phrase quickly and smoothly. Emphasize the words or syllables highlighted in red. A strikethrough means don't pronounce that letter.

• Learn to string together words or phrases to create many more phrases.

• Draw your own pictures to help with memorization and pronunciation.

Note: This book may produce Americanized German.

For free sound bytes, visit slanguage.com.

GREETINGS

Hello
Hallo

Hall Oh

Welcome
Willkommen

Vil Comb In

Good morning
Guten Morgen

Goo 10 Morgan

Good evening
Guten Abend

Goo 10 Ah Bend

What is your name?
Wie heißen sie?

Vee Highs An Zee?

What is his name?
Wie heißt er?

Vee Heist Air?

How are you?
Wie gehts?

Vee Gates?

Are you well?
Gehts dir gut?

Gates Deer Good?

I'm fine
Es geht mir gut

Ess Get Mirror Good

Good health!
Zum Wohl!

Zoom Vole!

Mister
Herr

Hair

Please
Bitte

Bitta

Take your place
Nehmen sie Platz

Neigh Men Zee Plots

Thank you very much
Danke schön

Dunk a Shoe'n

FAMILY

Son *Sohn*	**Zone**
Uncle *Onkel*	**Uncle**
Parents *Eltern*	**Elton**
Granddaughter *Enkelin*	**Ankle In**

Wedding *Hochzeit*	**Hoch Site**
Wedding dress *Brautkleid*	**Brought Clyde**
Couple *Paar*	**Par**
Descendant *Abkömmling*	**Of Come Link**

Member
Mitglied

Mitt Glee'd

Person
Person

Pair Zone

Baby
Baby

Baby

Guest
Gast

Gust

PLACES TO GO

Hotel
Hotel

Hotel

Restaurant
Restaurant

Restaurant

Train station
Bahnhof

Bun Oaf

Airport
Flughafen

Fluke Huffin

Bank
Bonk

Bonk

Cafeteria
Cafeteria

Cough Feet a Rita

Fortress
Festung

Fess Tongue

Hospital
Krankenhaus

Krunkin House

Mosque
Moschee

Mo She

Embassy
Botschaft

Boat Shaft

Park
Park

Pock

Movie theater
Kino

Key No

FOOD AND RESTAURANTS

I'd like . . .
Ich möchte . . .

Ick Mocha . . .

Beer
Bier

Beer

Coffee
Kaffee

Coffee

Chicken
Huhn

Who'n

Pork
Schwein

Sh'Vine

Locks

Salmon
Lachs

Broccoli
Broccoli

Bro Coal Lee

French fries
Pommes frites

Pump Fr'eats

Plate
Teller

Teller

Glass
Glas

Glass

Peas
Erbsen

Absent

Potato
Kartoffel

Car Toe Full

Rice
Reis

Butter
Butter

Egg
Ei

Toast
Toast

Rice

Boot Er

Eye

Toast

Sandwich
Sandwich

Sandwich

Dessert
Dessert

Dessert

Ice cream
Eis

Ice

Apple
Apfel

App Full

To drink *Trinken*	**Drinkin'**
Spoon *Löffel*	**Low Full**
To bite *Beißen*	**Bison**
Cabbage *Kohl*	**Coal**

Sweet *Süß*	**Zeus**
Salt *Salz*	**Salts**
Salty *Salzig*	**Salt Sick**
Eggplant *Aubergine*	**Ah Bargain**

Banana
Banane

Banana

Cranberry
Moosbeere

Moose Beer

Melon
Melone

May Low Knee

Orange
Orange

Orange

Avocado *Avocado*	**Avocado**
Noodle *Nudel*	**Noodle**
Yummy *Lecker*	**Liquor**
Delicious *Köstlich*	**Coast Lick**

TRANSPORTATION

Flight
Flug

Fluke

Seat
Platz

Plots

To land
Landen

London

Departure
Abfahrt

Up Fart

Jet
Jet

Jet

Ticket
Fahrkarte

Far Cart

To tow
Schleppen

Shleppin'

Cart
Karren

Car In

Bus
Bus

Bus

Traffic light
Ampel

Ample

Van
Kleinbus

Kline Bus

Car
Auto

Auto

Seat belt *Sicherheitsgurt*	 **Scissor Heights Good**
Gasoline *Benzin*	**Ben Seen**
To park *Parken*	**Pockin**
Horn *Hupe*	**Hoop a**

LABOR

Lawyer *Anwalt*	**An Vault**
Cook *Koch*	**Coke**
Doctor *Doktor*	**Doctor**
Florist *Blumenhändler*	**Bloomin' Handler**

Female flight attendant
Flugbegleiterin

Fluke Be Gliderin'

Pilot
Pilot

Pee Low't

Policemen
Polizist

Pole Eat Cyst

Baker
Bäcker

Becker

Garbageman *Müllmann*	**Mull Men**
Philosopher *Philosoph*	**Fee Low's Oaf**
Journalist *Journalist*	**Journalist**
Soldier *Soldat*	**Sole Dot**

ADJECTIVES AND ADVERBS

New
Neu

Noy

Free
Frei

Fry

Full
Voll

Foal

Useless
Nutzlos

Newt Slows

Big
Groß

Gross

Fat
Fett

Fet

Young
Jung

Young

Thin
Dünn

Done

Small
Klein

Kline

Charming
Anmutig

An Moo Tick

Nice
Nett

Net

Blond
Blond

Blond

Stupid
Dumm

Dumb

Poor
Arm

Arm

Lazy
Faul

Foul

Patient
Geduldig

Get Dual Dig

Funny *Lustig*	**Loose Tick**

Popular *Populär*	**Pope Poo Lair**

Frank *Offen*	**Off Inn**

Courteous *Zuvorkommend*	**Zoo 4 Comment**

Idiotic	**Edie Oh Tish**
Idiotisch	

Childish	**Kin Dish**
Kindisch	

Tired	**Mood**
Müde	

Sick	**Krunk**
Krank	

Cold
Kalt

Cult

Hard
Hart

Heart

Smooth
Glatt

Glut

Quite
Ganz

Guns

Then
Dann

Don

Maybe
Eventuell

Event 2 Well

In the middle
Mitten in

Mitten Inn

Never
Nie

Knee

To the left
Links

Links

Patiently
Geduldig

Gay Duel Dick

Less
Weniger

Vinegar

Fluently
Fließend

Flea Send

Slowly
Langsam

Land Sum

Quickly
Flugs

Flukes

VERBS

To be
Sein

Sign

To find
Finden

Fin Den

To do
Tun

Tune

To have to
Müssen

Moose Inn

To send
Senden

Zen Den

Knee Men

To take
Nehmen

To cover
Abdecken

Up Deckin'

Fee Gun

To sweep
Fegen

To offer
Anbieten

Ann Bee 10

To use
Benutzen

Ben Nuts An

To bring
Bringen

Bringin'

To hope
Hoffen

Huffin'

To depend
Abhängen

Up Hangin'

Shoots Inn

To protect
Schützen

To forbid
Verbieten

Fair Bee 10

To complain
Sich beklagen

Sick Be Clog'n

To deceive
Täuschen

Toy Shen

To stay
Bleiben

Bly Ben

To move
Bewegen

Bee Vegan

To push
Schieben

She Ben

To lift
Heben

Hay Ben

Comb In

To come
Kommen

To rot
Verfaulen

Fair Fallen

MONEY AND SHOPPING

Credit card *Kreditkarte*	**Cred Eat Cart**
Dollar *Dollar*	**Dollar**
Newsstand *Zeitungskiosk*	**Sightin' Kiosk**
Flea market *Flohmarkt*	**Flow Marked**

Pastry shop
Konditorei

Cone Dee Tore Eye

Price
Preis

Price

Credit
Kredit

Cred Eat

To cost
Kosten

Costin'

Hat *Hut*	**Hoot**
Blouse *Bluse*	**Blues**
Pair *Paar*	**Par**
Sneakers *Turnschuhe*	**Turn Shoe**

Ring *Ring*	**Ring**
Raincoat *Regenmantel*	**Reagan Mantle**
Jeans *Jeans*	**Jeans**
Skirt *Rock*	**Rock**

Sweater
Pullover

Pull Over

Dress
Kleid

Clyde

Shorts
Kurze Hosen

Curt's Hosen

T-shirt
T-Shirt

T-shirt

Slipper
Hausschuh

House Shoe

Bracelet
Armband

Arm Band

Cap
Kappe

Cap

Sandals
Sandalen

Zen Doll An

HEALTH AND HYGIENE

Mouth
Mund

Moon'd

Arm
Arm

Arm

Knee
Knie

K'Knee

Leg
Bein

Bye'n

Ear
Ohr

Oar

Neck
Nacken

Knockin'

Skin
Haut

How't

Finger
Finger

Finger

Chin
Kinn

Kin

Forehead
Stirn

Stern

Sick
Krank

Krunk

Flu
Grippe

Grip

Medicine *Medizin*	**Met a Scene**
To cough *Husten*	**Houston**
Doctor *Arzt*	**Art'st**
To yawn *Gähnen*	**Keenin'**

To inhale
Inhalieren

Inn Heil Ear Un

Shampoo
Shampoo

Shampoo

Blood test
Bluttest

Blue Test

Bandage
Verband

Fair Bunt

| Virus | **Veer Us** |
| *Virus* | |

| Disease | **Krunk Height** |
| *Krankheit* | |

| Infection | **Infection** |
| *Infektion* | |

| Shock | **Shock** |
| *Schock* | |

HOUSEHOLD

House
Haus

House

Table
Tisch

Tish

Telephone
Telefon

Telephone

Bed
Bett

Bet

Refrigerator
Kühlschrank

Cool Shrunk

Sofa
Sofa

Sofa

Bench
Bank

Bonk

Video
Video

Video

Picture *Bild*	**Built**
Restroom *Toilette*	 **Toy Let**
Photo *Foto*	**Photo**
Housework *Hausarbeit*	**House a Bite**

Corridor
Korridor

Corridor

Pillow
Kissen

Kissin'

Curtain
Vorhang

4 Hung

Elevator
Lift

Lift

PLANTS, ANIMALS, AND NATURE

Fire
Feuer

Foyer

Ice
Eis

Ice

Sun
Sonne

Zone

Rock
Fels

Fells

Lake
See

Zee

Flower
Blume

Bloom

Bush
Busch

Bush

Rose
Rose

Rose

Poppy
Mohn

Moan

Palm tree
Palme

Palm

Seaweed
Seetang

Zee Tongue

Lotus flower
Lotusblume

Lotus Bloom

Fish
Fisch

Cat
Katze

Mouse
Maus

Goose
Gans

Fish

Cats

Mouse

Guns

Shark
Hai

Hi

Insect
Insekt

Insect

Liquid
Flüssigkeit

Flu Sick Kite

Clay
Ton

Tone

ARTICLES, PRONOUNS, PREPOSITIONS, AND CONJUNCTIONS

A
Ein

Eye'n

You
Sie

Zee

She
Sie

Zee

We
Wir

Veer

They *Sie*	**Zee**
All *Alles*	**Alice**
If *Wenn*	**Venn**
Because *Weil*	**Vial**

With
Mit

Mitt

In
In

Inn

In front of
Vor

4

Around
Um

Um

| Without | **Own** |
| Ohne | |

| How | **Vee** |
| Wie | |

| From | **Fun** |
| Von | |

EDUCATION

Computer
Computer

Computer

Library
Bibliothek

Bib Lee Oh Tech

Experiment
Experiment

Experiment

Sum
Summe

Zoom

To solve
Lösen

Losin'

Mathematics
Mathematik

Matt a Matt Teak

Physics
Physik

Fizz Zeke

Grammar
Grammatik

Grammatic

Plus *Plus*	**Plus**
Minus *Minus*	**Me Nose**
Economics *Ökonomie*	**Oh Cone Oh Me**
Computer science *Informatik*	**Inn 4 Matt Tick**

NUMBERS AND TIME

One
Eins

Eye'ns

Two
Zwei

Z'Vie

Three
Drei

Dry

Four
Vier

Fear

Eleven *Elf*	**Elf**
Thirty *Dreißig*	**Dry Sick**
Million *Million*	**Mealy Own**
Billion *Milliarde*	**Mealy Yard**

Noon *Mittag*	 **Mitt Tog**
The past *Die Vergangenheit*	**Dee Fur Gangin' Height**
Evening *Abend*	**Ah Bend**
Holiday *Feiertag*	**Fire Tock**

Month *Monat*	**Moe Not**
Morning *Morgen*	**Morgan**
Day *Tag*	**Tock**
Minute *Minute*	**Me Newt**

Night
Nacht

Knocked

Tomorrow
Morgen

Morgan

GERMENGLISH

All these words (and many more) are identical in spelling and meaning in English and German. Although you may experience small slanguage pronunciation differences, you will still be understood.

- Angst
- Apartment
- Aspirin
- Auto
- Avocado
- Baby
- Ball
- Baseball
- Basketball
- Blond
- Broccoli
- Cafeteria
- Clown
- Computer
- Cookbook
- Dessert
- Diesel
- Elegant
- Experiment
- Fallen
- Film
- Finger
- Fit
- Football
- Glass
- Glitzy
- Golden
- Golf
- Hamburger
- Hammer
- Hotel
- In
- Intolerant
- Jeans
- Jogging
- Kiosk
- Mango
- Museum
- Nickel
- Noodle
- Orange
- Pizza
- Plus
- Pretzel
- Pullover
- Quartz
- Restaurant
- Ring
- Rugby
- Sandwich
- Sofa
- Tennis
- T-shirt
- Video
- Zigzag